Real Estate Investing

To order additional copies, please contact us.
BookSurge, LLC
www.booksurge.com
1-866-308-6235
orders@booksurge.com

JON
PETREEKO

REAL ESTATE
INVESTING
SMART FROM THE START

2003

Real Estate Investing

TABLE OF CONTENTS

This book is dedicated to my wife, Robbin Petreeko.

INTRODUCTION

- Do you seek a comprehensive way to achieve your real estate investing goals?
- Do you feel like you're on "information overload" with all of the real estate investing techniques available from various authors and experts?
- Do you wish someone would take you from start to finish without leaving out all of the important details along the way?
- Do you want to maximize your rate of return while guaranteeing the best chances of appreciation?
- Do you want to find so many deals that you don't know what to do with them?
- Do you wish someone would start you off with the easiest way to acquire an investment property...then continue your education in a methodical manner upon your "personal level of interest"?

Face it, we're all at different stages of development in relation to our overall investment goals and objectives. Some of you might still be looking for the perfect "investment vehicle". Others might be looking for ways to supplement their current passive income in order to get out of the "rat race".

I'm assuming that if you're reading a book about real estate investing that you understand the reasons *why* you should be investing in real estate. If not, let's go over the basics:

- **Leverage**– maximizing the cash-on-cash return on investment for every dollar you put into a deal

- **Appreciation**– in addition to monthly cash flow you want to be able to maximize your chances of appreciation
- **Tax Advantages**– utilizing the benefits of a 1031 tax exchange (which allows you to roll-over the profits from one property into a "like-kind" higher valued property eliminating any capital gains taxes) and creating "phantom cash flow" through depreciation and writing off expenses (see your CPA for exact details*).

Again, these are just the basics but I wanted to make sure I had everyone on the same page. Let's go on to the reason why I started investing in real estate and see if you can relate.

I came from a hard working middle class family. I started out working in "corporate America" because I felt like this was the only way I was going to achieve my financial objectives. I longed for a six-figure job with great benefits so I could enjoy the **American Dream**. I wanted to buy the fancy cars, big screen TV's, and numerous "liabilities" we all love!

I reached this level of success and you know what happened? I was getting in debt even though I was making what seemed like a lot of money! I had everything I wanted for now but my *financial future* looked pretty dismal. How much money did I have to make in order to achieve my goals of **financial freedom**? I had to change my thinking and I had to do it fast.

I was instantly attracted to real estate investing for all of the benefits we listed before and even more importantly:

- **9 out of 10 millionaires achieve their status by investing or holding their assets in real estate**

This is a very powerful and true statement! I knew I had to find out everything there was to know about the topic. I needed to develop my own **learning path** in order to benefit from all of the information available on real estate investing.

What I found was pretty frustrating and confusing. There was a ton of content but no real direction. I started looking at techniques like no money down, lease purchase, flipping, buy and hold, foreclosures, tax liens, etc.

These are all great strategies but I wanted to start with something that would build up my *foundation of knowledge*. I needed to start off with the basic principles that would make me successful in any real estate investing strategy that I wanted to incorporate!

This sounded really easy but it wasn't! It took numerous failures encountered along the way for me to finally come up with a logical strategy for one avenue of real estate investing. Here are the basics of this strategy:

- **Find a property in an area that is most likely to appreciate**
- **Purchase the property based on a simple formula allowing for the best possible rate of return and lowest risk factors possible**
- **Let your team manage the majority of the operations involved with the property while you find other deals**
- **Evaluate your market place on a quarterly basis in order to develop an "exit strategy" for your property or properties**
- **Sell your property or properties while the related market place is at its peak value maximizing appreciation expectations**
- **Continue this cycle until you decide on pursuing another real estate investing strategy or use this strategy to acquire the level of wealth you desire**

The amazing part is that it really is that **simple**. The hardest part is knowing where to start. You need to capture all of the information and **steps** along the way in order to succeed. This is where I come in. My goal is to give you the most comprehensive methods and techniques available allowing you to achieve your dreams in the fastest way possible.

I know what you're thinking:

- "I have a full-time job. When am I going to have time to invest?"
- "I have a family and kids. Can this work for me too?"
- "I don't have much money and my credit is not very good either".
- "Real estate is risky. I think I'm better off investing in something else".

I'm going to say this once...Everyone can do it! I felt the same way you might be feeling right now:

- Depressed
- Frustrated
- Angry
- Confused
- Overwhelmed
- Doubtful
- Fearful

That's the main reason I wrote this book. If I can help out as many people as possible on this "very broad" topic I will have accomplished my goal. I know exactly all of the thoughts going through your mind—I've had them all, and that is why we can relate. You'll make many decisions in your life but take advantage of this opportunity.

"Real Estate Investing Smart from the Start"© **is designed to take you to the next step in the most comprehensive way possible. I know you're feeling motivated so let's get started...**

Where do I start?

This answer typically depends on where you are right at this very moment. Think clearly about how you would answer the following questions:

- How much do you have to invest?
- Do you have basic financial literacy?
- Do you have the time to dedicate to increasing your real estate investing skills through constant learning and improvement?
- Why do you want to do it in the first place?

The fact of the matter is that you have to **outline your future goals** and start thinking about the reasons why you need to accomplish them. Is it for financial freedom or just to "sock away" some extra money for your children's college fund while enjoying the benefits of a (hopefully) appreciating asset? How serious you think about these answers will help dictate whether you can take the risk necessary to *significantly increase your net worth.* **I vote for financial freedom** but I'm going to start this off from square one so everyone feels comfortable in moving forward with the first step. If you feel more advanced than "square one" I suggest you start from here anyway. I overlooked so many things along the way because I truly thought that I did everything 100% correct from the start. I made so many minor stupid mistakes that I would not want to see anyone face the same set-backs.

See everything from here with an open mind and you will truly succeed. You first have to believe in yourself and sometimes that is the hardest thing to do. Believe me, I've been there. I've been a victim of self-doubt, stubbornness, and just plain negativity in general. I blamed everyone else for my lack of knowledge in finding the proper resources when attempting to acquire an investment property. *Everyone told me what to do but they didn't lead me to the* "**best resources!**"

I wanted options if things went wrong. I wanted to be resourceful when I really needed to get a deal done fast. I wanted to find deals on a daily, weekly, and monthly basis but more importantly…I wanted to know exactly what I needed to do when the opportunity presented itself. We will get right to the first step once I give you a better idea of how this book will be an ideal learning tool for your future utilization.

Let's start with the set-up. I break every part of acquiring an investment property into sections or steps. I'll be filling in the "fine print" details that everyone forgets to tell you about. We will be going over some "**true stories of failure and success**" that I encountered through my earlier days of investing. I want you to feel every bit of emotion that hit me, but more importantly I want you to learn from my mistakes! The format will be ideal for learning and strategizing.

I will start off with a brief description of the particular **step** or part of acquiring an investment property. For example; in one section we will talk about *lenders* and what they analyze when considering you for a loan. Good credit or no credit. Where there's a will there's a way!

Then I will go over exactly what you need to look for and how to go about it. I will go through the gruesome details and give you as much information as possible so you can avoid wasting time and effort.

My goal is to walk you through each phase of acquiring an investment property with the easiest directions possible.

Throughout the book I will give you numerous resources that I utilize in my continuous hunt for investment properties.

I will also be including "**quotes of supreme importance**" at the end of each chapter to give you added motivation and a little something to think about while reading through the book. They will all be based on *important principles to remember* when investing in real estate.

I know you're excited so let's get to it!

Why Would You Want to Read Another Book About Real Estate Investing?

Since I started fully researching every piece of information I could get my hands on about the topic a few years ago I believe I have learned a tremendous amount. But with the abundance of ideas and concepts available about this subject I feel that many beginners, like myself at one time, have been led into a world of **information overload!** I found my head going in a hundred different directions trying to apply every principle while working a full-time job. I wanted a "step-by-step guide" to lead me in the right direction. I wanted someone to be there for me when I totally screwed something up or when I applied bad advice to a particular aspect of real estate investing.

I've been frustrated, pissed-off, and almost ready to **"throw in the towel"** on many occasions. Why didn't I? Stubbornness and the burning desire to succeed! That was part of it but not the only reason. I was willing to fall many times in order to learn from my mistakes. *I wanted someone to tell me about all the mistakes I shouldn't have made in the first place and teach me how to correct the ones I'd already made.*

I knew plenty of great resources for teaching myself to become a better real estate investor but I really wish I had someone "telling me stories from the trenches!" *I wanted someone to give me the good, the bad & the ugly without any sugar coating.* I knew I could capture every vital step in acquiring an investment property and relating it to a past experience I learned from. I wanted to give a beginner every story I had…pouring my guts into everything I did wrong and how

I prevailed. I wanted to give them descriptive details on the exact **"failures, successes, and future resources to avoid the failures from happening again"**...all in that order!

So I wrote a book, a guide, and created a system giving a beginning real estate investor my sweat, blood, and tears. I have a passion for this subject and I hope to reach thousands and even millions of people who could benefit from my "time in the trenches!"

So if you're ready to get started and see things with an open mind, please turn to Chapter One. You're in for quite a journey...

CHAPTER 1

Location is everything?

Do you agree with that statement? If you don't you're in for a big surprise because I believe that this is one of the **most important** aspects to consider before investing in a property! But it's not all about location. Timing is a crucial factor and we will cover this extensively later on in the chapter. "Where do I look?" is what most people ask me. I think they should be asking me *why do I look* in a specific area?"

We all invest in real estate because we're aware of the benefits available including: appreciation, tax advantages, cash flow, return on investment, etc., etc. What I ask is *how do I maximize these benefits*...specifically return on investment and appreciation?

Have you ever heard of **economic data** and **key market indicators**? This is how I compile all of the factors to decide whether I will invest in a specific market place or not. I know what you're thinking...give me an example. Let's break this down a step further. Every market in the world experiences periods of "boom and bust". We'll demonstrate using stages:

- During stage 1 the market is depressed and near "rock bottom". Most sellers are motivated and bargains are found everywhere

- During stage 2 the prices are increasing slowly and steadily. There are periods of growth from new jobs coming to the area and expansion from the efforts of the economic development boards within each town, county, state, etc.
- During stage 3 the market peaks and prices seem almost "outrageous" and unjustified! I'm sure there are quite a few people out there that live in areas that are in stage 3 and you're thinking the same way I am; how did this get so out of control? It really comes down to *"supply and demand"*.

So without going into a long drawn-out conversation about economics and census reports let's talk about how we're going to get ahead of the game by knowing *how to determine where to invest!*. What stage do we want to invest in? If you're thinking smart you want to invest in stage 1 where *prices are low and bargains are found* on a daily, weekly, and monthly basis.

This is the stage where you can maximize your **"cash on cash investment"** and benefit tremendously from the future appreciation expectations and estimates. I know what you're thinking…where do I find areas in stage 1? We find markets in stage 1 based on the following key indicators:

- **existing home sales**
- **notices of default and "foreclosure sales"**
- **new home building permits**
- **interest rates**

All of the above key indicators are influenced by market forces of *supply and demand.* This is the same way that the U.S. Dept. of Commerce tracks how well the economy is doing. We utilize the indicators to track how each market place is doing. We want **existing home sales** to be at a low or just starting to increase. We want **notices of default** and **foreclosure sales** to be at a high and just starting to show signs of slowing down and improvement. We want **new home building permits** to be at a low but just starting to increase at a gradual pace. We want **interest rates** to be low in order to capitalize on maximizing our return on investment.

I know that this is starting to sound a little confusing but this is where your learning begins. I suggest you get educated on the following topics: **economics** and **analyzing specific important data!** This is how you will get successful – but how does analyzing specific important data fit in here? This is **everything!**

Let's take a real world example and guide you though it...

Steps for Researching a Market Place

In this section we're going to be covering an important investing technique that most beginners are not aware of...researching a market place to determine the future appreciation estimates/ expectations. This will be based on numerous factors.

Let's use Kansas City, Missouri for example. Your goal is to find out *everything* that can stimulate a growth in population. Remember, you have to think supply and demand. You want to consider the following factors:

- **Population (present—10 year estimates)**
- **Cost of living**
- **Business climate comparison**
- **Local unemployment rate**
- **Existing home sales**

- Foreclosures and notices of default
- New home building permits
- Interest rates (current average)
  Go to: http://www.ecodevdirectory.com

Before you begin you should know the county (in this case it's Jackson County for KC, MO) and obviously the city and state as well! Your best place to begin is at the "state economic development board" websites. Here are some great examples:

Missouri Economic Development Council
http://www.showme.org/cgi-bin/c.cgi?intro.html
Missouri Dept. Economic Development
http://www.ecodev.state.mo.us

Next, you want to move on to the local "economic development board" websites.

Here are some additional examples for Kansas City:

Kansas City Economic Development
http://www.edckc.com
Kansas City Area Development Council
http://www.smartkc.com
Jackson Co. Economic Development
http://www.jacksongov.org

Then you want to move on to the website for the city of Kansas City, MO:

http://www.kcmo.org

From all of the above sites you will be able to find out statistics on everything imaginable including many basic economic indicators! You will cover the following as a brief example:

- Proposed budget for spending on specific projects/ capital improvements, etc.
- Business developments, initiatives, corporate relocation efforts, cost of living, crime rates, unemployment rate

- Economic momentum, inflation rates, population

The list goes on and on but I'm sure you can see how this will help in your market analysis in the market place of your choice. This is just one example.

If you really want to master this stuff I suggest you maximize 2 resources:

http://wwww.narei.com
http://www.realestatetiming.com

Marc Stephen Garrison and Robert Campbell do an amazing job of using market analysis to their advantage when searching for real estate. They stay "ahead of the game" because they go through the research necessary in order to truly maximize appreciation. They have entire books dedicated to the importance of *location* and *market timing*. Mr. Campbell even has a great software program out that helps you match up the right data to track a market place based on the same basic economic indicators we just went over in this chapter!

MY PERSONAL STORY OF FAILURE AND SUCCESS

When I started looking for my first investment property I took the recommendation of many authors, and only looked in my own territory...or no more than 2 hours outside of it. I looked every single weekend in the papers. I checked tons of online resources but I had a hard time finding a property that met my 30%+ return on investment goals.

I was very frustrated and ready to give up when I started reading about economic indicators and market analysis. I never thought about the idea before but it really made sense so I devoured every piece of information I could find about these subjects. I was enthusiastic and ready to start! This spark of energy and excitement was what made the difference in me "just doing it" instead of quitting all together.

This isn't a typical story of failure for the fact that I didn't do anything particularly stupid or wrong. But I really did contemplate quitting. Just this fact alone is frightening, because I really don't know what else I would rather be doing right now. This was when I knew I was bit by the "bug" of real estate investing. Will you see real estate investing with the same passion I do? Who knows? I know that I don't regret it one bit and I'm glad that I could tell this story with faith and confidence. I took the fear of quitting and losing and turned it into a burning desire and passion for making it work. On that note I leave you with 3 different quotes on faith from Napoleon Hill:

QUOTES FOR THE CHAPTER:

"Faith is the eternal elixir which gives life, power and action to the impulse of thought!"
"Faith is the starting point of all accumulation of riches!"
"Faith is the only known antidote for failure!"
—Napoleon Hill

CHAPTER 2

Find and Analyze Deals Everywhere with the Proper Tools

What are the proper tools? You've gone through the tedious process of analyzing the economic climate within a market-place. You may have even identified numerous market-places that fit your investment strategy. How do you locate properties that will give the best possible rate of return?

Let's review the mission statement for this book so we stay focused on the ultimate goal:

"Real Estate Investing Smart from the Start© is a system that shows a person how to purchase investment properties with maximum cash flow and higher-than-average appreciation indicators."

You need to have automatic "leads" sent to you on a daily basis. We'll get into the specifics of setting up your automatic lead sources in the upcoming chapter on real estate brokers. In conjunction, you need to search for investment properties through your own efforts. Some of the best deals I ever found were through my own searching, *and every single one of them was found on the internet!*

If you don't think deals can be found on a daily basis through the internet then you haven't looked hard enough. I'm going to make this a little bit easier for you. At the end of this chapter I'm going to give you a list of the best websites out there that advertise investment properties specifically for real estate investors!

When I'm searching for properties I keep it as simple and automated as possible.

I identify the key #'s (asking price, monthly rental income) first. I weed out the ones that don't fall within the 100 to 1 ratio.

For example:

Asking price= $100,000

Monthly rental income= $1,000

That may sound outrageous but those are my minimum standards. I seek properties that give me at least a 30% cash on cash return on investment! I can do this by searching in the right spots. Let me tell you that you're not going to find these properties just sitting back waiting for them to appear. They are equivalent to **hidden treasures** waiting for someone to snatch them up! You're going to have to look at a lot of properties in order to narrow down the best potential deals. It's as simple as that.

You need to dedicate time on a daily basis to do this. I suggest 1 hour minimum per day to start. A lot of time will be wasted analyzing and sorting through the "rubble" in order to find a "diamond in the rough". You will even go a few days without finding anything or finding only a couple showing potential. Go back and review the chapter on location after reading this book. *You have to make this as systematic as possible, and learning to identify weaknesses during the due diligence process will help you achieve success the quickest.*

By prospecting for leads on a daily basis you will become an expert at identifying traits of great deals. Don't become frustrated because most of them will come back with something wrong. You may not even find out until weeks later. Let me give you an example so you know what I'm talking about:

You find a 3 BR condo in a great market-place that's producing about a 33% return on investment. During the *due diligence process* you find out that the property is in "worst shape than expected". The owner discloses (after you sign a preliminary sales contract) that a couple of items need to be repaired (dishwasher, AC unit, etc.). You want him to pay for the repairs but he isn't budging on the price. These new added expenses will throw off your "cash on cash return on investment" goals. You don't get a good vibe after dealing with the owner on this issue and expect that there could be future conflicts.

If you get a bad gut feeling it's usually right! Don't be afraid to move on and find a better deal. Your goal is to analyze and find the best properties possible. You may have to turn down a few good ones in order to capitalize on a "great deal", but believe me, it's worth it. Persistence, patience, and timing are of the essence when practicing this system. Don't lose focus of the ultimate goal and make your decisions wisely. Here are some of the websites that can make your search for investment properties much easier. ***Remember, this is another tool for finding the best investment properties possible...not an "end-all solution!"***

www.realtor.com

This site is general but it's really improved quite a bit over the years and it allows you to completely customize your searches. I use this one to occasionally locate deals but it works best for checking out "comps" in the area. The site allows you to *see what properties are selling for* within a specific market place helping to determine if you're getting the best price possible!

I have listed a bunch of other sites below similar to this one. Some are betters than others but they all allow you to analyze more properties in the least amount of time possible:

www.homescout.com

www.homegain.com

www.househunt.com

***

www.ree.com

I could spend days at this last site. This site specializes in **real estate exchanges** and it's really interesting to see what other investors have in their portfolios. This is a great place to email owners inquiring about their available properties. You will find that many of them are investors as well so they are more familiar with creative deals (owner financing, holding a note for the majority of the sales price, etc.). Some owners are extremely motivated while others are just looking to consolidate their investments. Other owners are looking to get rid of smaller, under-performing assets and move it into larger properties. You will find a ton of properties in this site. Spend a good hour or so going through it and let me know what you think. I almost always find something of interest here!

www.owners.com

This is a "**for sale by owner**" site. You will notice a lot of these types of sites listed below as well. You have to get in the habit of searching here for bargains. You may waste some time but its well worth it when you find a deal that fits your investment strategy. Check out the following sites as well:

www.byowners.com

www.forsalebyowner.com

www.privateforsale.com

www.fsbo.com

***

www.creonline.com

You will notice that this site doesn't allow property searches. Why do I have it in here? It's a great resource for finding motivated sellers or other investors looking to liquidate their properties. Look under one section here though, **classifieds.** Every now and then I find a really good deal here. Again, you will notice more creative/ flexible terms here. Some people have assumable mortgages (the lender allows an outside party to take over the payments if qualified), and others are just looking to liquidate fast. They know that investors are always on the site searching!

www.reidepot.com

This site has a couple of really interesting forums. Go to the **Real Estate Classified forum** on a daily basis. Every now and then you will find a good deal and if not...they have tons of aggressive lenders advertising or promoting there all the time. Here's another resource for you when searching for a loan!

www.realestateinvesting.com

Go to **Search Community** and look under Property Listings. Every now and then you can find some good deals here. Most of the visitors are investors and you can definitely find some creative deals here. Check it out and let me know what you think.

QUOTES FOR THE CHAPTER:

"The most intelligent man living cannot succeed in accumulating money...
nor in any other undertaking...without plans which are practical and workable."
"Temporary defeat should mean only one thing, the

certain knowledge that there is something wrong with
your plan."
—Napoleon Hill

CHAPTER 3

Cash Flow Formula and the Basics for a Good Deal

This is one aspect of investing that you have to make as routine and *automated* as possible. It's going to take some work though because you have to be able to easily identify potential cash flow properties strictly by looking at some rough numbers. The easiest way to accomplish this is to use the following basic preliminary formula for determining if the property will be a favorable return on investment or not:

- **100 X the monthly rental income = total purchase price or less**

Seems pretty basic, right? The amazing part is that *it's pretty accurate* depending on what part of the country you're in. This can vary depending on different cost of living levels... raising or lowering expenses like taxes, insurance, interest rates, etc. For example; in states like Tennessee and Missouri the cost of living levels are extremely low compared to New York and New Jersey. This makes it easier for you to find "cash flow" properties in areas with a low cost of living! Write this down. By tracking and identifying market places that combine a low cost of living with an expanding workforce...you will always be *ahead of the game*.

Let me show you an example of a **5 Step Winning**

Formula for determining if a property will be a favorable investment no matter where you're looking:

1. Use the **preliminary formula** to run the rough numbers

2. Use an investment analysis sheet or the following **hot resource** link below for determining the actual #'s by factoring in your monthly expenses (taxes, insurance, property management, closing costs, etc.) and factoring in an appropriate vacancy rate (we will go into this in more depth later on in the chapter):

   http://www.richdad.com/realestate

3. Call or email and get more details on the property. Find out what area of town it's in. Ask for comparables or "comps". Ask if any work needs to be done. Ask what work has been done to the house (upgrades, renovations, etc.). Run the police reports for the area.

4. If the house is located out of town ask the real estate agent to take pictures and email or fax them over so you could take a look at the property itself and the neighborhood as well

5. Prepare an offer!

Now as you probably have noticed we left out quite a bit of detailed info along with the "**5 Step Winning Formula**". More importantly, let's take a step back and make this process a whole lot easier for you by having "other experts in their field" *bringing you deals to the table.* This is where we get to the real hardcore true life information that you need to know in order to become successful in investing and starting/operating a business in general:

● **Building Your Team!**

I know what you're saying.........this sounds like a difficult task! Well, it's not really that hard if you break it down into **steps** and *start identifying* specific parts of your team. In the next chapter we're going to start identifying "key players" on your team and how to make them work for you in the most productive way possible! We're going to start with...

QUOTE FOR THE CHAPTER:

"With few exceptions, the man who cannot follow a leader intelligently, cannot become an efficient leader."
—Napoleon Hill

CHAPTER 4

Organizing Your "Dream Team" with the Proper Advisors and Mentors

You've decided on a location. You're utilizing the proper tools to find an income property that meets your **return on investment goals**. Now let's move on to the "make it or break it" part of your plan...putting the team together!

Let's start with the *key members* of your team and how they specifically play a part in your success:

Real Estate Broker (Realtor)

You will deal with quite a few real estate brokers over the course of your career. You should be looking for someone who can assist with specific "search criteria" requirements. Here is the most common problem you will run into with most real estate brokers across the nation:

- **Lack of follow up**

This is really common but don't worry. You have to be persistent and honest from the start. Talk to them about your specific goals and make sure they're aware of the fact that you plan on doing more deals with them...as long as they keep sending you potential investment properties. Most of the brokers I work with have me on an "auto-responder" list within their website, email manager or database. I wake up in the morning, and I have listings from agents in all the market places I want to invest in! We'll go into this in more detail in the next chapter specifically covering real estate brokers.

Just think of real estate brokers as your recruiters. They make your job easier by bringing you warm leads on a steady basis. The more recruiters, the more warm leads you have, and the more warm leads you have, the better chance you're going to find a property within your search criteria! My minimum "cash on cash" return on investment standards are:

30 – 35%

You'd be surprised. It's not as hard as you think to find properties within this criteria.

Let's move on to the next critical advisors which are...

Mortgage Broker (lender)

Let's take this broad category and make it easier to work with. Remember, our goal is to buy and hold properties for maximum appreciation and cash flow. We're not going to cover more advanced techniques such as "flipping", "wholesaling", "pre-foreclosures", etc. so there will be no need to discuss hard money lenders here.

We're looking for traditional mortgage brokers who can match your financial statement with a lender who sees you as a good candidate for one of their loan programs. You need to be up front about 2 major items:

- **Your credit score**
- **Your financial statement**

Have your credit score ran by any of the major companies (Experian, **www.experian.com**), (Equifax, **www.equifax.com**), etc. Tell the mortgage broker your credit score but tell him that you have one major request...do not let anyone pull up your credit scores for any reason! Make your broker tell each prospective lender that assume that my client's credit score is *"whatever is it."* It's not hard to do and if the lender needs a reason, no problem. Have your broker state that "my client is conscious and accountable with his/her finances, and does not want to create excess inquiries on his/her credit which will lower his/her overall score."

A lender will respect this and factor the initial decision based on the # given. My failure story at the end of this chapter has to do with "excess inquiries" so you'll see why I'm so adamant about this topic!

On to the importance of producing your own financial statement. If you have never done this don't worry...you have tons of resources that will make this job easier than you expect. I hate doing my financial statement but I do realize the importance of having this information updated on a monthly basis. It displays your **financial health** and it also shows a perspective lender that you are more accountable than 98% of the people out there! This is a bonus so don't overlook this important step. We'll discuss this in more detail in the chapter dedicated to mortgage brokers later on in the book. Let's move on to...

Property Manager

This is one of the most important advisors in my opinion—especially being an out-of-state investor. Again, going back to my main objective for investing outside of my own state which is:

"To maximize appreciation and cash flow by investing in market places that are positioned for rapid growth and expansion over a definitive time frame."

I'm not going to go into a ton of detail here because the section of the book dedicated to property management is *power-packed* with info you just can't miss. It will literally save you thousands of dollars and eliminate your time being wasted.

I will tell you that *property management should be factored into each property's business plan from the start.* Too many beginning investors forget about this then find themselves "in a hole" when they don't get the return on investment they expected.

The *key players* have been defined for your advisor team. Let's move on to the little known experts that you should identify before locking down any sales contract within a specific market place.

Home Inspector

No matter what anyone tells you always make your sales contracts contingent upon a satisfactory home inspection and leave yourself an "escape clause" in case excessive damage is found and repairs are needed.

Home inspectors will help eliminate properties that don't fit into your **overall investment strategy**. I can't tell you how many times this has happened. The property looks great on the inside and outside and it falls within my return on investment guidelines. I lock down a sales contract and then find out that there are excessive damages and the property needs numerous minor repairs. I have a couple of choices:

- I could walk away from the property, receive my earnest deposit money back, and accept my loss of $200-500 (home inspection expenses depending on the property size, etc.)
- I could negotiate with the seller and make them fix every single thing that has been addressed on the home inspection report

What do you do here? It's really up to you and each individual deal will dictate a different potential outcome. The point I'm trying to make is that you wouldn't have these options and you wouldn't be "protected" if you didn't have a home inspector analyze the property in the first place. **Don't** try to save money by not utilizing this very important advisor. You may end up buying a lemon and you won't know until it's too late. Also, don't forget to make sure your legal advisor protects you with an appropriate clause so you can walk away from the property if you don't feel comfortable with the necessary repairs. You will always feel better *"walking away" with a $350 loss instead of a $35,000 liability down the road!* Make this a part of your exit strategy in each property's business plan. You just never know and you must be prepared for anything!

Attorney

A lot of beginners will try and save money and avoid hiring an attorney to assist them in their real estate ventures. This is a big mistake. The expense is well worth it! Consult with an attorney who specializes in real estate. Your ideal selection should invest in real estate as well. I learn so much every time I talk to my attorneys!

I've studied the basics but law is extremely complex! If I "feed off" just a little bit of their knowledge I will be in a much better position for future deals. I work with a couple of different attorneys because I invest almost completely out of my own state. What I found is that many attorneys (specialized or not) are only licensed in the state they represent. This can be a problem when dealing with real estate. An attorney based out of Missouri will not be liable for handling a property you're looking to acquire in Tennessee!

This is one of the reasons why I like the Pre-Paid Legal Services group (www.prepaidlegal.com). When you have a specific opportunity out of state...you call your primary representative and they will refer you to a local attorney in their network that can assist. You even save 25% off the price by using one of their network providers!

Whatever way you decide to handle the selection of a competent attorney…make sure you have proper representation in the state where you're looking for properties. The laws vary so much in different states that you will not know the differences without proper legal assistance.

IMPORTANT TIP:

Make sure your legal advisor handles all of your contracts, paperwork, etc. when investing in real estate.*

Accountant (CPA)

When we mentioned some of the core benefits of why we invest in real estate in the first place…you probably noticed "tax benefits". This is a big one and you will not be able to take advantage of the tax benefits without having a capable accountant on your team of advisors. You may be able to get away with doing the accounting work yourself with only 1 or 2 properties but this task is best left to the professionals. Taxes, just like laws, are changing all the time and you shouldn't waste your efforts trying to learn everything "new" about this broad topic. I personally keep up to date with everything Diane Kennedy of http://www.taxloopholes.com/ has to say but I leave the main stuff to my CPA. You will make your CPA's life much easier if you learn to utilize an accounting software program like QuickBooks®. I use QuickBooks® personally and let me tell you that it is a savior! QuickBooks® allows you to input & itemize all of your income, expenses, and any other items related to your investment properties.

Your CPA can ask for a quick summary of reports (balance sheet, income versus expenses, etc.), and you have the ability to print them out with the click of a button. I document all of my expenses, income, etc. in QuickBooks® but I always keep a "back-up" copy of any receipts, payments, etc. in case of an audit. You need to be accountable and prepared to show where all of your income and expenses come from. This is extremely important! Make sure this advisor is part of your team. They will save you more money than you ever thought possible and their services are a legitimate "write-off" as well. You can't go wrong.

Let's sum up the benefits of your advisors. Your CPA, just like every other one of your advisors...*should be ready and willing to help you with any issues*! you should be able to contact any one of your advisors and ask them a question. You should have a strong relationship with your advisors. They are responsible for many of your business affairs. They will also be a source of knowledge and inspiration when you really don't know what to do in a specific situation. You can't get by successfully without them and they should be one of your most powerful assets.

Make sure to network around when putting together your team of advisors. Don't be afraid to interview numerous advisors before choosing the right ones. You may even have to use a couple of advisors before deciding on your "final team". Just like in pro sports; it may take a while to put together a winning team. You can't give up and you always have to be "on the look out" for the best players. Remember that the truly successful people in real estate are in it for the *long haul*. The sooner you put together your winning roster of advisors...the sooner you will reach your ultimate goals!

Let's discuss mentors because this is something not enough beginners take seriously. I was guilty of this myself at the start, and I don't want to see you missing out on this important piece of the puzzle!

Mentors

Mentors are something you have to take advantage of *as early as possible*! There are so many people out there willing to share their experiences and knowledge with you. You just have to find these people. It doesn't sound easy but it really is. It's going to require some work and effort on your part but the sacrifice will be well worth it. Let's explore some potential avenues for finding mentors:

- **Investor association meetings/ events**

Almost anywhere in the nation within a one-hour drive you should be spending one day a week at an investor meeting. Most of the investor groups meet once a week in the evenings or during a day on the weekend. I know what you're thinking; I'm just a beginner with limited knowledge. I'm a little intimidated. Are they really going to take me seriously?

Guess what…you are the most likely candidate for receiving help from members of an investor group! We all had to start somewhere. Other investors realize this and they're not afraid to share information and experiences with you because they understand the frustration and confusion you're experiencing as a beginner. Go into the meeting and be honest about your current level of education, development, experience, and goals. You won't believe how many people will be receptive to your plans. Most of the investor associations cost under $100 per year to become a member. *You will have the benefit of listening to other investors share their experiences, successes & failures with you.* This benefit alone is a priceless asset you can't take for granted!

Check out the resources section in the back of the book to locate a few websites that will help you locate investor associations in your area. I will be adding this feature to my website, **www.reismart.com**, in the near future so check-in from time to time and take advantage of this search tool.

Another great way to find a mentor is through the use of:

- **Forums**

I can't tell you how many times I have found a mentor through a real estate investing forum. Most of the times the dialogue will stem from an email on a question I have asked of a specific "expert in their field". Check out the resources section in the back of the book for my comments on the best forums for you to utilize immediately. This again is going to require some work and effort on your part. Some people will never get back to you for one reason or another. You have to be persistent and keep at it. The people who respond and help you out in one way or another are looking to share their knowledge with you!

Do you know how many people have done this with me? I'm eager to help someone out because I know how it was to be a beginner experiencing **information overload.** Again, I'm one of *many people out there who* will do this! Just don't abuse the right. Many "experts in their field" are extremely busy professionals and they just don't have the time to answer numerous emails on a daily or even weekly basis. Know your limits. Always be professional, business-like, and respectful when communicating via email or over the phone. You never know who you'll network with that can be a vital contact for future deals, information, or just someone to run something by!

The last tip we're going to cover for finding mentors is through:

- **Seminars/ Boot-camps**

I've met tons of other investors at daily seminars and boot-camps. This is a great place to learn and network. Go to these events with an open mind and a positive attitude. You never know who you'll meet and how they can help you out. I seek out evening or weekend seminars about a specific topic of interest through the Learning Annex (which hosts speakers on various topics of real estate and almost anything else in general.) The Learning Annex is located in many major cities but other companies/organizations offer these same types of learning seminars. Go to www.learningannex.com and find out if there's one located near your city. I owe a lot of my success to this organization. They provide a great service for an investor or business professional at any level of development!

The easiest way to succeed is to find someone who's "been there, done that". It's not as hard as you think but it will require effort, patience and persistence on your end. You can do it but don't wait long. It will only delay you in achieving your ultimate goals!

QUOTE FOR THE CHAPTER:

"Without doubt, the most common weakness of all human beings is the habit of leaving their minds open to the negative influence of other people."
-Napoleon Hill

This quote reiterates how important it is to have an advisor team and mentors that support your ideas and goals 100%. We all have enough negative influences being "thrown at us" while we're going through our daily routines. You must stay focused on your game plan and not let these negative influences dampen your attitude and desire to succeed.

Let's move along to the next chapter on...

CHAPTER 5

Real Estate Brokers…Giving Them Your Search Criteria and Having Them Locate Deals for You

I don't know how many times people have asked me: "Where do you find so many deals, and how do you find enough resources to analyze hundreds of properties on a consistent basis?" My answer is simple: I don't have the time to do this and I would rather have qualified professionals bringing me deals on a consistent basis!

Real estate brokers are one of the keys to your success. The hardest part is establishing a relationship with a group of qualified professionals that understand your goals and objectives. I want to break this process down step-by-step so you understand exactly what I'm talking about because not enough investors are doing this.

Let's say you have identified a market place that is primed for growth. You have done everything from the chapter on location earlier in the book and you're ready to make the next move. How do you start? Here is exactly what I do and let's use Jacksonville, FL as an example market place.

- Go to http://www.google.com/ and search under the category of **Jacksonville, FL real estate—and—Jacksonville, FL investment properties**

- These 2 searches will pull up numerous real estate companies in the Jacksonville, FL area

- Search for real estate professionals/ companies that cater to **investors** first
- Search for real estate professionals/ companies that cater to **buyers** next
- Put together a "template" email stating your *goals, objectives*, and *search criteria*
- Take the "template" email and send it to as many realtors as possible that cater to **investors** or **buyers** (if this is less than 10 total contacts/companies, than send some to other realtors in the area as well…you never know!)
- Follow up with each contact if you don't hear back from them or wait for them to get back to you within a 3-6 day time frame (RE brokers are busy people)
- Make sure you stress to them the fact that you analyze hundreds of properties on a weekly basis and not to get frustrated if we can't locate a deal within the first few months
- Watch your warm leads flow to your email on a daily and weekly basis and "analyze away"…narrowing down the best deals possible

This is a broad description of events if you don't know what I'm referring to so I'm going to show you exactly what one of the emails I send out looks like:

Jean Roberts,
I have an interest in establishing a relationship with you and your company. I'm an out-of-state investor looking to purchase a group of properties in the Kansas City, MO market-place within the next 6-12 months. My corporation has a definitive search criteria and game plan. We would like you to send us all property listings

within the criteria on a daily basis in order to complete our evaluation process. We value your time and efforts so we will only be responding to properties that fall within our stringent criteria. We require your patience because it may take a little while before we find a property that meets our expectations. Please be persistent in sending us listings and don't get frustrated. Our goal is to form a mutually beneficial relationship where we can both prosper and help each other out. We would like to discuss the search criteria in more detail and ask you some questions in specific about Kansas City, MO as well. I look forward to your follow up and enjoy the rest of your day!

Sincerely,

Jon Petreeko care of Creative Real Estate Ventures, LLC

Now, what does this template email accomplish? First off, you are identifying yourself in a professional, business-like manner. You are establishing ground rules and expectations from the beginning so there are no "guessing games". You are letting the real estate broker know that you're serious about your intentions, and you expect him or her to be serious about their efforts as well. You are not promising anything but you are letting them know about the potential for business with you and your company. You are looking for them to follow up with you and discuss the search criteria in more detail. You are also telling them that you need their assistance

In some questions about the market-place itself. Here are some of the questions you should ask:

- What areas (of the market-place) do you see increasing in value? Why?
- Can you get crime reports if necessary?
- Can you pull-up school reports if necessary?
- Can you send listings for motivated sellers?
- Do you work with any other investors currently?
- Do you have a specialty? Fixer-uppers? Investor flips, etc.?
- How long have you been working in this market-place?

This is what will happen. If you send out 15 emails, maybe 1/2 will respond. This is o.k. You want to "weed out" the brokers that aren't serious. Your ideal goal is to find 2-5 brokers that:

- *Work with other investors*
- *Specialize in working with investors*
- *Display professionalism and excellent customer service*
- *Are hungry to gain your business and respect*
- *Will be persistent in their efforts and understanding of your objectives*

This is easier said than done but it's really not that hard to do! You just have to incorporate a game plan and follow-up strategy. If you're confident in what you want to achieve other people will recognize this quality as well. They will become attracted to you and want to do business with you. It's a simple fact. You have to let other people know that you are "for real"! Make real estate brokers part of your "team" and you will succeed. You can't do this alone. The more support you have from this continuous "lead-generating" resource the easier it will be to achieve your real estate investing goals!

IMPORTANT TIP:

I recommend that you open up a separate free email account such as hotmail or any other similar provider for all of your real estate activities. This will help you stay organized. It will also keep business and personal emails from merging which could create confusion. I set up folders in my free email account for organizing all of the types of emails to make things easier. For example; I keep all of my research on a market place in a folder, potential deals in another folder, and important broker/advisor correspondence in yet another folder. This is your key to organization. Working on multiple deals and working with multiple contacts at one time can become overwhelming and time consuming. You need a system in place for making this as easy as possible!

It's now time to discuss mortgage brokers and how they fit on your team. They can make your life a piece of cake but you're going to have to show them that you're accountable and trustworthy. You can do this so let me show you how...

QUOTE FOR THE CHAPTER:

"Opportunities are usually disguised as hard work, so most people don't recognize them."
Ann Landers

CHAPTER 6

Lenders...What Type and How You Can Partner with Them for Future Gains and Effortless Closing Cycles

The first step you *must take* before prospecting for potential lenders is conducting a *self-evaluation, which is* described in more detail in the next section below. I wanted to go over this information *twice* as a reminder of how **important** is truly is!

After the self-evaluation you must determine what lender will work best with your specific loan request. My suggestion is to utilize a mortgage broker that will be *aggressive* and shop your loan request to numerous lenders...making your life easier and giving you a better chance of obtaining the money you need in order to *close the deal!*

The best approach is being extremely honest **right up front** about your overall financial condition and credit score. The initial phone call or e-mail will allow the mortgage broker to determine which lender will work best with your specific individual situation. You will be *amazed* at how much respect you'll receive when you display this level of professionalism. Mortgage brokers enjoy working with an **organized, honest & accountable** person. It makes their jobs easier and they will work harder to get you the loan!

IMPORTANT TIP:

If you want to go a step farther and make an extremely memorable impression on a mortgage broker tell them about your **overall game plan**!

If they see an opportunity for you to be a steady client who can give them "residual commission" you will win their support and you'll also be incorporating an important lesson in becoming *financially free.* . developing your team of advisors. This is and should be a major part of your **overall game plan**!

Let's go over your self-evaluation so we could determine where to start...

Where are you now? (Self-evaluation)

This section is so important because it truly helps you determine where you need to start. I have people asking me all of the time:

- Where do you find the most aggressive lenders that will work with investors requiring creative terms & conditions along with high loan to value ratios?
- What if my credit score is low?
- I don't have any assets to claim. Will they still work with me on getting a loan?

I'll be honest with you: I can't answer any of these questions without analyzing your personal financial statement and credit report. This will allow me to get you started in the right direction. What I will tell you is that there are quite a few lenders out there and with the right amount of searching... you'll find one that will work with you (no matter how bad your situation may be).

Let's get this process started so I need you to answer the following questions:

- Have you ever completed a personal financial statement?

- Do you know what your credit score is?
- Have you ever had a consultant review your credit report for errors, discrepancies, etc.?
- Do you know how your FICO score is determined?
- Do you know what a bank/lender will consider as collateral (personal possessions/ car, jewelry, etc.)?
- Do you know what a mortgage broker will require when first evaluating if you qualify for one of their loan programs?

I can go on forever but I think you know where I'm going here. If you answered "no" to the majority of these questions I recommend that you work on increasing your financial literacy skills. In the meantime, I'm going to make it easier for you to work with prospective lenders. I'm going to let you know exactly what you need to have prepared when seeking a loan. This section is going to make your life easier and it's going to create a "system" enabling you to minimize wasted time on future real estate transactions.

I have the following documents prepared with every loan package I send out:

- **Last 2 years of tax returns**
- **Past 2 months of pay stubs**
- **Past 2 months of bank statements (checking, savings, money market, business acct.'s, etc.)**
- **401k, IRA, stock option plan, pension fund statements (all pages)**
- **Financial statement**
- **Credit report (most recent)**
- **Mortgage payment statement on primary residence (if applicable)**

- Proof of insurance for primary residence (if applicable)

- Copy of divorce papers (if applicable)

- Schedule of real estate owned (equity compared to debt owed…if applicable)

- Schedules of businesses owned (fair market value along with financial statement…if applicable)

As you can see this is a very long list of documents! Some lenders will require even more information but it's usually unlikely. Is this a pain in the butt? Of course it is but *it's necessary when they're performing their "due diligence" on you!*

It's all about the level of risk in their eyes. With the rates so low and the volume of loans, refinances, etc. so high… lenders can become extremely picky with their selections. No lender wants to deal with foreclosures and late payment issues. The more accountable you can present yourself to a mortgage broker…the easier it will be for them to "shop your loan"!

Let me share with you exactly what I do when sending out a loan packet:

1. I have all of our (my wife and I) tax return data (last 2 years) in a PDF file on my computer. I email this to the lender in order to avoid extra paperwork and to make both of our lives easier

2. I make copies of our last 2 months bank statement (business, checking, money market, savings, etc.)

3. I make copies of our most updated 401k statements, IRA's, employee stock option plans, etc.

4. I create an updated financial statement and send them our latest credit reports

5. I send over a list of updated schedule of real estate and businesses owned

6. I send over a copy of our primary residence's mortgage payment booklet & proof of insurance

Now I have a system in place for organizing all of the items above. I paper clip each section together and label them with a "yellow post-it note" making it easier for the mortgage broker to review my data. I put the packet together in a professional folder with an attractive cover page (usually a template for the corporation I will hold the real estate in). This will attract a mortgage broker's attention because the majority of the people they deal with on a daily basis are "not accountable". You will look like a shining star with a professional, organized packet of information increasing your chances of getting a loan! Follow this system and you will make everyone's life much easier.

IMPORTANT TIP:

Remember to tell your mortgage broker that you do not want potential lenders to ever "pull your credit report". Make it contingent upon the number you give them or the credit report you send in your packet. Read my failure and success story below and you'll see what I mean.

MY STORY OF FAILURE & SUCCESS

I hate telling this story because to be honest...I really didn't see it coming. I had been investing a little over a year and then all of a sudden I received a call from a lender I was trying to close a loan with. The lender stated that the underwriting dept. (the dept. that reviews all of the details of your loan from front to back) noticed an excessive amount of inquiries on my credit report. There were almost 100 inquiries on my credit report over the course of a year and change! I thought back to all of the different companies that may have looked at my credit score when reviewing my file for a loan. I saw the following areas where I was seeking or closing on a loan within the one-year time frame:

- Primary residence (purchase & refinance)
- Car loans
- Credit card machine
- Investment properties

These were the "biggie" categories but I had found the major problem. I was working with 2-3 different mortgage brokers at one time to close on a commercial property. *What I didn't know was that 2 out of the 3 brokers were shopping my loan to over 50 different lenders!* That's where all of the damn inquiries came from.

This is how I turned a failure into a success:

Going forward, I established ground rules from square one with each mortgage broker I was working with. I made sure that they never allowed a lender to pull up my credit score when going through the initial due diligence process pre-qualifying me for a loan request. I made sure that I addressed this issue with any other potential companies that may pull my credit for some reason (car loan, credit card companies, equity line, etc.). I also worked with a credit repair company to eliminate any flaws in my credit. I suggest doing this especially if your credit score is under 700. The company I work with is http://www.academycredit.com/. Mention affiliate number 1126 and they will give you a discount!

I hope this lesson helps you out. It was a great learning experience for me!

QUOTE FOR THE CHAPTER:

"All it takes is a dream, a team, and a theme to create a stream of perpetual income."
—Robert Allen

CHAPTER 7

Property Management Companies...Make Sure the Relationship and Expectations are Established from Day 1

In this chapter we're going to cover how important it is to utilize a "competent" property management company to handle your investment properties. We already know how vital it is to have a property management company as part of your "team" (after discussing this topic in an earlier chapter.) They're your eyes and ears for all of the daily activities associated with owning an investment property.

Some of you may be thinking that it's much easier to handle this responsibility on your own. You can *save quite a bit of money* by managing the property yourself. Most property management companies charge 8-10% of the monthly rental income. This can really "cut into" cash flow and reduce your overall net income! You are absolutely right. But you're forgetting the #1 reason why you want to invest in real estate in the first place...to eliminate the need for another job by **creating passive income**! You don't want to create another *job* for yourself. Your goal is to delegate as much of the "day-to day activities" to a competent professional.

If your game plan includes acquiring more than 10 income properties...how are you going to manage them yourself?

Do you want to manage *every responsibility* your investment properties will require? Let's break this down further and go over the **common tasks** you will be responsible for by not utilizing a property management company*:

- collecting rent(s)
- collecting late payments and other associated penalty fees (returned checks, maintenance expenses, property damage, etc.)
- answering maintenance calls on a 24/7 basis
- coordinating maintenance requests with the appropriate local contractors/vendors
- inspecting the property when a tenant moves out
- inspecting the property when a tenant moves in
- advertising the property when it's vacant
- screening potential tenants
- showing the property to potential tenants
- finalizing contract details with tenants
- understanding local legal issues (eviction, various tenant conflicts, local city, state, and county laws, etc.)

This list is never-ending if you really want to cover every potential problem that *can occur* during the landlord/tenant relationship. Why would you want to go through the hassle of handling all of these responsibilities on your own? Your mind has more important things to worry about...like creating additional income streams!

Instead of trying to do this yourself...you should be factoring the monthly expense of a property manager into each individual property's **business plan**! The expense is tax deductible and the most important thing is...it's worth every penny! Your *time can be leveraged more appropriately* by finding new investing opportunities or learning about a new real estate investing technique. We do have some important things to address about property management companies. They're not all good and some can be downright horrible! How do we weed out the good from the bad? Let me give you an example.

You've gone through the standard "due diligence process". The property you're interested in has met your investing goals and you're just about to place an offer. You need to make sure that a local management company can handle the property for you. Here is what I suggest:

INTERVIEW AT LEAST 3 PROPERTY MANAGEMENT COMPANIES OVER THE PHONE

Here's the information you want to give them:

- Type and specific location of property
- Logistics of how many bedrooms, baths, sq. ft., etc.
- Monthly gross rental income

After giving them this information sit back and let them tell you more about their company. Make sure you cover the following during your initial conversation:

% management fee per month

Specifically what this covers (in writing preferably)

Date established for when the rent check is due

See if they are flexible—some of my tenants pay on the 1st of the month and others pay on the 15th depending on their individual pay schedules

Grace period after due date

Some companies will allow 1-2 days after the due date just in case the check is running late/ most will assess a "late fee"—find out how much their late fee is and make sure they notify the tenants when they make an introduction call

Schedule of fees

Make sure you know what the late payment penalties are and how much they cost. Most property management companies typically charge from $25-75 depending where you are in the country.

What will make your life much easier is if a property management company has a prospectus and/or a sample contract listing all of their services, costs, terms and conditions, etc. It's always a great idea to have your attorney review this before making any final decisions. You can never be *too safe* with this!

IMPORTANT TIP:

You should have an attorney review every document in relation to the property management contract...specifically terms and conditions. For an ideal scenario an attorney should review every document associated with a real estate transaction. Make sure you don't "skimp out" on this particular action item, because you think it just cuts into cash flow! It's well worth it in the long run. To make any real *major money* in real estate you need to be in the game for the long term with a ***well thought-out, definitive plan***.

MY PERSONAL STORY OF FAILURE AND SUCCESS

Here's a perfect "learning experience" for you. I had run into a situation with a property I acquired in Kansas City, MO. It was my very first investment property and I thought it would save me some money to manage the property on my own...from out of state and over 3 hours away by plane! It was a clean 1 BR/ 1 BA condo in a quiet subdivision about 20 minutes from central KC, MO.

I picked it up for $25k. The owner held a note for $20k @ 6% amortized over 10 years. I put $5k down. It created about $100 per month in net income after the mortgage and all expenses. It wasn't a "cash cow" but it was a great starter property that provided some amazing learning experiences. I wanted to maximize my "passive income" in the least time possible so I decided to save money by not hiring a property management company.

Here's what happened. The local realtor agreed to show the property to potential tenants if I paid her a set commission of $400. I provided the advertising in a local popular newspaper classifieds section. Then I would have the prospective tenant call the local realtor once I screened them through a toll-free voice mail system I had set up through the ad.

Well, she got frustrated when she was "stood up" by potential tenants a couple of times, and she didn't want to be involved any longer. I was stupid for not having her sign a service contract defining all of the terms and conditions. I was stuck with a property that was presently sitting vacant for a little over 3 months! This was killing my cash flow and financial estimates indefinitely. So listen to what happens next!

I was frantic to get the property rented so I called a local property management company. I signed a contract with them the same day within the same hour after we initially spoke. I read through their materials quickly because I wanted to get them started ASAP. Instead of understanding the relationship right off the bat I assumed that they knew what they were doing, and that they would tell me exactly what to do! This company turned out to be an absolute nightmare.

- **The person responsible for getting the unit rented failed to show up for an appointment with the same tenant two days in a row**

- **They spent hundreds of dollars on advertising and never followed up on calls made by tenants requesting an appointment to see the unit**

- **They didn't return phone calls for 2-3 days on issues that required attention**

- We fought back and forth over the phone about topics that weren't addressed "UP FRONT"

Let me remind you that I didn't call 3 different companies as recommended earlier in this chapter. I also didn't find out enough information about the company. I was lazy and guilty of not performing the proper "due diligence". I saw a problem. I wanted to get it fixed ASAP but I didn't analyze the situation properly.

Let's summarize what we've learned from my personal example and this entire chapter:

- Competent property management companies perform a specialized duty allowing you to spend *your time* more efficiently
- Competent property management companies have the *resources*, the *time*, and the *skills* to manage an investment property better than you can...especially if you are investing from out-of-state
- *Always factor* a property management expense into an investment property's financial statement
- A competent property management company is a *valuable member of your team*...allowing you to focus on your overall investment goals instead of wasting energy on items and issues that require constant attention and worrying
- *Research* and *interview* at least 3 property management companies within a specific region—this will help you determine the best "fit" for your team
- Property management companies *make a real estate investors life much easier*...it's really that simple

HOW DO I APPLY THIS INTO MY OVERALL INVESTING STRATEGY?

HOW DID I TURN MY FAILURE INTO A SUCCESS?

We all make mistakes. Take responsibility for your actions and analyze the situation appropriately with other members of your team. Learn from your mistakes and discuss them with other members of your team. How did I learn from my failure? Here is what I did:

I interviewed 4 other Kansas City-based property management companies over the phone. I weeded out 2 companies after performing some further due diligence. I found a company whose president was also a real estate investor. I interviewed him personally. I told him specifically about the problems that occurred with the initial property management company. We established ground rules and communication from day 1. We still have a relationship to this day! He has also opened up other opportunities for me because he "understood my goals and objections". I told him my personal game plan and he's been a member of my team ever since we spoke!

QUOTE FOR THE CHAPTER:

"To be a successful real estate investor you must delegate tasks to the
appropriate member(s) of your team. The better you become at finding competent members for your team, the more money you will make!"
—Jon Petreeko

CHAPTER 8

Traits of Successful People

I want this chapter to be an enlightening experience for everyone so I've broken it down into 5 sections:

- Foundation & Plan
- Habits
- Continuing Education & Personal Development
- Team Building
- Assessment & Review (self-test)

FOUNDATION & PLAN

I don't know how many people out there have read self-help or self-improvement books but never made the initiative and "took the first step". What is the first step? This book is about real estate investing but the bigger picture takes us back to *financial literacy*. How financially literate are you currently? Can you fill out a personal financial statement? Have you put together a personal game plan as of yet?

I know what you're thinking. What a hassle! How do I know where I'm going when I don't even know what I want to do? The initial **self-analysis** is critical because it creates a vision for your future. You will ultimately dictate if this vision is positive or negative. If you don't take any advice from this book please listen to what I have to say and put it into action immediately. Go purchase Napoleon Hill's "**Think and Grow Rich**". You must read this book at least 5-6 times while reviewing specific chapters and completing assignments (dictated by Napoleon Hill) on a daily, weekly, and monthly basis.

What? Believe me...I thought that this was a joke as well. What I realized is that everything in this book is 100% accurate. Human tendencies and habits are very predictable. It took me 6 months from the first time someone recommended this book to actually go and pick it up! Procrastination is one of the biggest factors leading to failure. Napoleon Hill spent his entire career analyzing human behavior and traits of successful people. You may not want to believe what he's discovered, but you can't dispel the truth behind it. He's a hero in my mind because he's created a system of success for me and any other people out there to follow. This system of success was developed based on research and case studies.

It has taken me so long to incorporate the strategies that Napoleon Hill recommends. It's not easy at all. He takes your every-day thoughts and actions and puts a complete "spin on them". You have to act and think differently in order to succeed. This is not something that comes overnight. It is achieved through constant practice, attention and reinforcement. It won't be easy and it won't be fun at first...but the end results are greater than you can ever imagine!

Start out by incorporating a personal game plan. This should include anything that you plan on doing to improve yourself over the next: 6 months, 1 year, 2 years, 5 years, and 10 years. This initial plan may take you a month or so to complete but spend at least 30 minutes a day on refining this **overall**

game plan. Don't ever give up and put this plan into writing. Rehearse it numerous times so it becomes "engraved" in your memory bank. If you need more help on taking this first step please email me at: **sales@reismart.com** so I could offer some additional support depending on your specific situation.

The next step will be to read "Think & Grow Rich" by Napoleon Hill. Re-read it until it becomes "engraved" in your memory bank. Highlight sentences in the book that really "hit home", and write down these sentences on a separate sheet of paper. These sentences will be your inspiration and positive reinforcement going forward. They will also help you understand key portions of the book in your own personal learning style. Incorporate the principles that he recommends. Complete the assignments he recommends. After this you will be ready for...

HABITS

Repeat after me. We all have bad habits. Some of us have more bad habits than others. I still have bad habits to this day that I work on improving constantly. Habits are not easy to break. Most of us go our whole lives believing our routines and everyday activities are productive and fruitful. John Beaman, a friend and Rich Dad coach, taught me so much on the topic of habits and time management. A good majority of the stuff John taught me I didn't want to believe. Do you know why? It was a different way of thinking and I was reluctant to change and even more reluctant to change my habits!

If you want to achieve success in the least amount of time possible you have to identify weaknesses in your daily habits and work on improving them through consistency and positive reinforcement. I'll give you an example:

During one of our sessions I noted to John that I felt

like my time was really limited, because I had 3 different businesses going along with my real estate investing activities and corporate job. We focused on time management. We itemized every single day of the week and broke down each activity into a "timed event". I had to be accountable for everything I was doing 24 hours a day, 7 days a week. Do you think I loved this idea? I didn't want to believe it at first but he showed me a technique that I still use to this day.

John told me to purchase a quality, digital voice recorder capable of downloading the content to a PC. During my commuting time I could take advantage of a *window of opportunity* I never saw before. I would focus on a different project each day and record my thoughts and ideas for this specific project. It could be a thought about an addition to the business plan or potentially a revised "mission statement". John advised me to take each project and break it down into an *action item time-line*…**giving as much detail as possible on how I would achieve my goals within this time-line**. This was not an easy task to focus on, but it worked wonders once I used this technique on a daily basis.

I then would keep each specific project in a separate folder/file (within the digital recorder) and record it on to a CD that I could listen to and critique. This allowed me to see which ideas I should put into "action" and which ideas just didn't make the cut. How many times have you been driving along daydreaming when a great thought or idea pops into your head? *Do you ever take action if you don't record or document this thought or idea?* Think about this.

The sooner *you identify weaknesses in your daily habits* and find ways to improve them…the sooner you will achieve success. Try it out. You'll see exactly what I mean. Let's talk about what's going to keep you from going *stale* and always staying "ahead of the pack".

CONTINUING EDUCATION & PERSONAL DEVELOPMENT

When I first started out I had absolutely no game plan. I just "gave it my all" and tried to constantly learn new things about financial literacy and real estate investing. While this worked for a while I knew that I had to develop a system that would allow me to **learn something about everything**. I had a sales & marketing background. This only got me so far. I suggest you learn about the following topics in order to maximize your chances of becoming a successful real estate investor:

- Financial Literacy
- Basic Accounting
- Corporations (LLC, S Corp, C Corp, LP, etc.)
- Sales & Marketing
- Negotiation
- Business Law
- Developing Systems
- Habits of Successful People

Make it a minimum to read at least a book per week on one of the topics above. Also, make sure to choose an author that you can relate to. I love the entire "Rich Dad Team of Advisors" because they offer something on every topic above! Review my recommended resources at the end of this book. I'm confident that you will be very happy with the results from the resources suggested.

TEAM BUILDING

Hang around with success, it's contagious. This is so true. Surround yourself with negative people and you will most likely pick up a negative attitude. Stay away from people that drag you down. One of your first priorities is developing your team. This is going to be a long and tedious task and it's almost never ending. As you develop and grow your asset column...you may notice your team changing. This is common. Your ideal goal is to have all of the members of your team in place. If you expand in a different direction...you just add a team member.

Do you know I still have not assembled my "dream team"? I'm very close, but I've out-grown certain members of my team already. This is not something that happens overnight. Some people have a "talent" for assembling a "dream team" in a short time frame, yet the majority of people in our society never even come close. Your team becomes your 2nd family when you achieve a specific level of success. They turn into people that you can call on when you have questions, problems, or you just want to discuss a potential opportunity. As your team expands and becomes more knowledgeable...the more you succeed! Your goal is to recruit the best advisors, mentors, and heroes. Make this an extremely critical "action item" and put it on your "to-do" list now!

Make it a 1-2 year goal to have recruited the best team of advisors and mentors around. This can be a slow process because in your learning process you will constantly add and delete members of your team. Remember to be persistent in your efforts. You can't settle for 2nd best, because your team of advisors and mentors will ultimately accelerate or decelerate your chances for success. I suggest you read some books by Robert Allen and become familiar with the "Mastermind" group concept. This concept will help you understand why your team is so important.

ASSESSMENT & REVIEW

What have you learned from this chapter that will benefit your real estate investing activities? With a **foundation** and **plan** you lay the groundwork for success. You have a defined plan that explains how you will reach your goals. You are incorporating better **habits** that will lead to success at a faster pace. With **continuing education** always a priority...your level of **personal development** will rise beyond your wildest expectations! By focusing on **team building**...you will constantly refine the members actively involved in your real estate investing activities. This will allow you to put your "dream team" together over a 1-2 year period.

You can do it! Just don't give up and be persistent in your actions. If you don't know something find it out. Don't just find it out...analyze it to death. Make sure you're constantly improving yourself and don't let "hard times" slow down your efforts. Excuses just hold you back and halt your efforts for achieving success. Make it a routine to constantly analyze your self. What areas of your game plan need improvement and what areas are at a satisfactory level? It's going to require a lot of work but it will be well worth every second!

QUOTE FOR THE CHAPTER:

"The story of the Three Little Pigs is more than a fairy tale. It is a story filled with truths. If you want to build a house of bricks you need good habits... for good habits are the bricks of the rich."
—Robert Kiyosaki

CHAPTER 9

Last Items of Due Diligence and Putting It All Together

L et's recap the entire system of finding a *winning investment property* from start to finish in the most logical format possible:

Understand the Basics of Financial Literacy

You must put together your own personal financial statement. You must understand the difference between assets & liabilities. You have to pull your credit report from any one of the major agencies (Experian, Equifax, etc.). You need to know how to read your FICO score and understand how it is determined (consult a credit repair specialist, http://www.academycredit.com/ if you need help). You must understand the basic criteria for determining cash flow on an investment property (Rental income– all expenses and debt cost from loans, etc.). You must construct your personal game plan to cover how you intend on reaching your goals over the next 6 months to 5 years. You should read the following books to help increase your level of financial literacy and proven success skill-sets:

- "Think & Grow Rich" by Napoleon Hill
- "Rich Dad Poor Dad" by Robert Kiyosaki

Research Market Places Offering Maximum Potential for Appreciation

In order to maximize your cash on cash return on investment for immediate cash flow and to increase your potential for future appreciation…you must conduct the proper market analysis. If you don't want to go through the hassle of doing this then you should follow the advice of someone who does go through the effort of conducting the proper market analysis. I suggest learning everything you can from both:

- **Marc Stephen Garrison of www.narei.com**
- **Robert Campbell of www.realestatetiming.com**

In my opinion, you should learn how to conduct the market analysis for any location you decide upon. This will help you identify future *expansion* market places and it will help you understand the true reasons *why* you should be investing there! Review the chapter on Locations over and over again until you understand the basics. When you understand the basics you can start performing the "hands-on" detailed market analysis. Again, it's really not that hard to do, but you have to incorporate these efforts into your overall game plan. By understanding what's going on in a specific area, you can evaluate that particular market place on a quarterly basis. When you understand key economic indicators you'll know exactly *when* you should liquidate your portfolio and move on to another *expansion* market place!

Start Organizing your "Dream Team"

Once you've decided on a market place or a bunch of market places you have to "lay the groundwork". This is not going to be an easy task, but the sooner you put your team together the quicker you'll achieve your goals. Remember who the key players are:

- **Real estate broker**
- **Mortgage broker**
- **Property Manager**

You also need to have your advisor team in place which include the following:

- **Home inspector**
- **Attorney**
- **CPA/ Tax Strategist**

The primary members of your team should be constantly feeding you leads and providing insight...while always looking out for your best interests. Your advisor team serves the same purpose. They are your guides and source of knowledge. You should be able to call on any member of your team at any time when you need a question or concern addressed. Again, it may take a while to construct your "dream team". The key is to constantly identify potential weaknesses and areas of strength. Your rolodex should be well-stocked and updated. You should be seeking mentors on a continuous basis as you develop. Never lose sight of your "true goals" and if you have any questions or concerns on anything...I suggest that you email me at: **sales@reismart.com** so I could work with you on finding potential solutions. Let's move on to the final step.

Daily Habits and Continuing Education

How are you ever going to achieve what I've just asked of you without changing your daily habits and making continuing education a daily "action item"? These are going to be the hardest things to grasp and follow. We are all set in our ways and I deal with stubbornness on a daily basis...unfortunately! You have to be able to identify your weaknesses and constantly find ways to improve them. Sometimes you will not be in the best environment to make this a reality every day. Don't worry. It's a long, consistent battle on the path to achieving your ultimate goals. Persistence is the key. You should focus on monitoring your progress to make sure you're in line with your overall "game plan" goals.

Your educational goals should also be in line with your overall "game plan". Applying continuing education should be a systematic and defined methodology. By mastering one technique first you can understand and incorporate the basics of real estate investing. You will be "prepped" or "prepared" for the next real estate investing technique with a foundation of knowledge! This one quote sums up how I feel about the importance of simplifying processes when attempting to achieve success:

QUOTE FOR THE CHAPTER:

"The most intelligent man living cannot succeed in accumulating money—nor in any other undertaking— without plans that are practical and workable. Just keep this fact in mind, and remember when your plans fail, that temporary defeat is not permanent failure. It may only mean that your plans have not been sound. Build other plans. Start all over again. Temporary defeat should mean only one thing, the certain knowledge that there is something wrong with your plan. Millions of men go through life in misery and poverty, because they lack a sound plan through which to accumulate a fortune. Your achievement can be no greater than your plans are sound."
—Napoleon Hill

CHAPTER 10

Final Words of Encouragement

When I first started learning about real estate investing, I *devoured* every bit of information I could find! I would read a full book every couple of days. The more I grasped the concepts, the more excited I became. My enthusiasm was racing and then I hit a wall called *frustration*. I was confused after reading so many different techniques of real estate investing; I didn't really know where to start, but I knew I had to do my first deal. I was passionate of the idea that real estate was going to be my ticket to financial freedom!

I wanted to master a technique that would provide me with the highest return on investment possible. I studied everything I could on the "buy and hold" technique of real estate investing. When combining the concept of buy and hold with maximum leverage (We rarely do any real estate transactions with any of our own money) I was able to develop a system that worked for me!

I was willing to wait 3-6 years maximum to become "wealthy" or truly financially free! Utilizing this real estate investing technique alone I will be on target to hit my goal! Now this required an aggressive game plan...and I'm ready to accomplish it! This is my personal story. What's yours going to be? Your answer may help determine how serious you are in getting out of the "rat race".

The point I'm trying to make is that anyone can accomplish their ultimate goals. How am I different from you? I don't have a college education and I came from a hard-working blue collar family. I didn't inherit money or win the lottery. It doesn't matter where anyone starts…it's where they ultimately end-up that means something!

We all develop a certain amount of strengths and weaknesses over the course of our lifetime. Some people have more things to work on than others. The key is identifying the weaknesses as soon as possible and finding ways to improve them. It sounds easier said than done. You're absolutely correct. That's why only 2% of the population reaches "millionaire status".

You have to start by mapping out a plan. If you want to achieve $2 million dollars in net worth within 5 years: how are you realistically going to do it? You want to include the most detail possible within the plan. It sounds extremely overwhelming, doesn't it? I felt the same way. It was a struggle for me to predict the future and put detailed description of what I was going to do. What it did do was paint a realistic picture of what I was willing…and not willing, to sacrifice. If you are willing to sacrifice and learn to correct your bad habits you will ultimately succeed in whatever you choose. I end this chapter off with a great quote from my friend and former Rich Dad Coach, John Beaman.

QUOTE FOR THE CHAPTER:

"The future of your success is hidden in your daily routine, these are called

habits. Men & women don't decide their future, men & women decide their
habits and their habits decide their future. You cannot change your future, until you change your habits."
—John Beaman

CHAPTER 11

Recommendations on Your "Must-have" Educational Resources for SUCCESS!

If you think just reading this book is going to take you where you need to be I'm afraid that you're mistaken. Real estate investing is ideally a long-term strategic plan where truly successful individuals are always finding new ways to make money through *continued education and mentoring.* We can't "know it all" so we must find ways to be more resourceful. You have to become a master at leveraging **your time** and **your money**!

This leads us to a chapter I am truly passionate about sharing with you! I wish I had this when I first started because it serves as a guide for anyone serious about achieving their real estate investing goals. If you don't re-read anything in my entire book please take the time to fully review this section and make copies if necessary!

This is how I'm going to break it down. I'm going to list a specific category, which will include books, websites, and forums that you absolutely cannot pass-up! These resources have been vital to my success and they will be for your success as well. Keep in mind that none of the resources I provide have any financial obligation to me in anyway. I don't believe in "sugar coating" anything and this is an extremely serious subject with me!

I only ask you to do one thing. When you find a resource

that has been *extremely beneficial* to you I want to know about it! Please send an email to: **sales@reismart.com**. I'm proud of what I've accomplished but my true goal is to satisfy **you...my customer for life** and the true indicator of my success! I know that you will enjoy them so here they are:

FINANCIAL LITERACY RESOURCES

http://www.richdad.com

Robert Kiyosaki has been a personal favorite of mine for a long time now. He helps people understand the basics of financial literacy and the habits of the rich in an easily comprehensible format. He offers various products and services that can benefit a beginning to advanced investor. I suggest the following because I have personally used them and benefited enormously:

Rich Dad Coaching

I had a chance to experience this first hand and let me tell you that it was "incredible". If you are serious at all about succeeding in business, real estate or any investing in general... this is a *must have.* I had the pleasure of working with John Beaman; a coach from the Rich Dad Organization. The Rich Dad staff gathers information on your current, personal situation before you sign up in order to verify that there will be a "proper fit" between the coach and student. The sessions last a total of 8 weeks but you have daily access to a toll-free hotline where willing and able Rich Dad coaching staff members answer any and all questions you could ever think of! Now where can you find a service like this? The cost is very reasonable for what you are get which is *priceless,* believe me!

Rich Dad Books and self-study kits:

I would recommend reading the entire line of Rich Dad books because I believe you will pick up something new in each one but if you have to only pick a few here are my personal recommendations:

Books:

- **Rich Dad Poor Dad (classic best seller)**
- **Guide to Investing**
- **Cash-flow Quadrant**
- **Prophecy**
  Self-study kits:
- **You Can Choose to be Rich (classic...an absolute must have*)**
- **Road to Riches: 6 Steps to Becoming a Successful Real Estate Investor (this one has loads of great ideas especially on the area of "due diligence"**

I would also recommend going to the Rich Dad forums and checking out specific areas of interest. When I want to find out about a particular real estate technique or I have a couple of questions that I don't have answers to...I always find great contacts through the Rich Dad Forums! You can meet many mentors and advisors this way. My last "hidden resource" from the Rich Dad site is a free real estate investment analysis tool located at the following link:

http://www.richdad.com/realestate

If you don't have the money to buy **real estate investment analysis software**...I suggest you use this free tool to start. It gives you the basics for determining if a property is a good investment. I used this tool to look at thousands of properties before upgrading to Dolf De Roos' REAP software found at:

http://www.dolfderoos.com

IMPORTANT TIP:

Just remember that any legal/professional service advice should be discussed again with a competent, certified advisor before making any final decisions. You can never be too careful and unfortunately there are people out there that give "*bad advice*" so be forewarned!

http://www.multiplestreamsofincome.com

Robert Allen has achieved a tremendous amount of success by building "powerful networks and streams of income" while helping other people achieve their dreams. He opens your eyes to the many ways you can make money in business and real estate ventures. His first major success was based around creative real estate or "no money down techniques". He has proven himself in numerous arenas and he still serves as a mentor to me to this day.

You have to read the following 2 books from Robert Allen:

- **Multiple Streams of Income**
- **One Minute Millionaire**

These books have been a source of inspiration for me as well as amazing resources and learning guides. Go to his various websites, sign up for his free newsletters and participate in his "free telephone seminars" to achieve success and development beyond your wildest dreams. He also has a coaching program available but I haven't attended personally so I can't give you any feedback on it.

Robert Allen is someone you want to learn from and constantly follow. Make sure he is part of your "educational path" for attaining wealth and success.

There are so many people out there writing about financial literacy but Robert Kiyosaki and Robert Allen are the best ones out there as far as I'm concerned. You will find many authors on this topic but you will see that they don't offer the amount of products, services, and support that these two can. If it turns out that "real estate" is not your deal keep working towards financial freedom by utilizing the expertise that Robert Kiyosaki and Robert Allen provide. You won't be sorry!

***

http://www.zeromillion.com

ZeroMillion.com is the businessperson and entrepreneur's bible. You won't believe all of the amazing resources available at your fingertips within this site! I suggest this site for anyone who is considering starting a business or even someone who currently has a business. You can network with contacts across the globe, read free newsletters, articles, and much, much more! They offer information on the following:

- **Business**

- **eBusiness**

- **Economics and Policy**

- **Entrepreneurship & young entrepreneurship**

- **Marketing & web marketing**

- **Personal Development**

Don't miss out on this vital resource and educational directory!

***

On to our next section which is a big one, **Real Estate**. You won't believe all of the information I have provided for you. Take it all to heart and let's get started...

<u>REAL ESTATE RESOURCES</u>

http://www.reitoolbelt.com

Darius Monsef has created a wonderful website that has tons of free resources and learning tools. The free articles from his list of participating "guru's of real estate" are something I check out on a weekly basis. His forums bring together some really talented people in the field of real estate and many of the questions posted are answered by the **experts themselves**! His site also offers free marketing samples, forms and contracts, web resources, real estate investing deal calculators, and much, much more!

***

http://www.creonline.com

J.P. Vaughn has a fantastic site providing a ton of extremely useful content. You can find loads of specialized articles written by numerous mentors in different areas of real estate investing. Subscribe to their newsletter and find out where all of the top real estate investing experts are speaking across the nation. They offer a lot of great educational resources such as books, kits, videos, etc. through their extremely talented network of real estate professionals. This is a top-notch site and I suggest you spend a ton of time here!

***

http://www.thecreativeinvestor.com

The creative investor or "TCI Investor" offers lots of free resources including:

- classified ads for investment properties
- a "University Program" where you can get the train-

ing needed to become a successful real estate investor and expand your current techniques in doing real estate transactions

- various forums for all levels of real estate investors
- free "how to" articles, special reports, downloads, etc.
- a great lender resource for residential, commercial, and hard money loans
- web links for finding contractors, property managers, other investors, etc.
- reviews on other real estate professionals' courses, books, etc.

This is a site that I still use on a daily and weekly basis. It offers some really good "bird-dogging" courses for beginning investors starting out with little cash and experience. Check this site out and visit it on a routine basis. You can't miss out on the information provided in one of the largest real estate investing online communities!

***

http://www.realestateinvesting.com

Make sure to sign up for their free newsletter. It's always packed with loads of beneficial information. Also, become a member of their site for free and take advantage of their various articles, special reports, and tons of great forums. They are another great resource that you should visit on a daily basis because you will learn something new every time you visit this site!

You can search for investment property listings, investor associations, and much more. The site is easy to navigate so I suggest you spend a lot of time here. You can't go wrong and

I personally use this site in my "arsenal" to constantly further my education on various real estate investor related topics!

***

http://www.uslandco.com

I love this site. They stress "financial freedom through real estate" and they truly stand behind this statement! I love the how-to articles and the "free leads" section of the site. I constantly receive emails from this company about investor events, boot camps, and daily workshops. They also keep me updated on new courses, books, free stuff, etc. They have great forums (like most of the sites listed here) so address questions and concerns with the online community and get closer to your goals on a daily and weekly basis!

***

IMPORTANT TIP:

Remember I mentioned earlier in the book how you must have "leads or deals" coming to you on a daily basis? This will help you evaluate hundreds and thousands of investment properties in order to "weed out" the true performers. It will also serve as great practice so the evaluation process is much less time consuming. Use the sites above and the real estate agent "tricks" mentioned earlier in the book as well to accomplish this "very important" task.

http://www.realestatepromo.com

This is really a "no frills" site but it offers great resources you can't pass up. Join their newsletter and receive a bonus eMini course & 3 special reports. You will find the following tools as well:

- **discussion groups**

- investment property listings
- articles and other resources
- investor clubs
- book and home study course listings and recommendations

Don't expect anything fancy on this site but it gets the job done and serves as another educational tool in your "arsenal"!

REAL ESTATE SPECIALIZED TOPICS
APPRECIATION & MARKET RESEARCH/ANALYSIS
EXPERTS

http://www.narei.com

Marc Stephen Garrison has been an inspiration for me since I saw him a few years ago at the Learning Annex in NYC. He opened my eyes to the importance of evaluating market places through specific techniques in order to maximize appreciation and overall cash flow.

Print out his articles on the "**FIFTH MIGRATION**" and the "**GARRISON CYCLE**". You will understand exactly what I'm talking about. He is an economics wiz and has plenty of experience with real estate. Become a member of his site for free and receive emails from him on a monthly basis that will help you succeed. You will receive "business expansion" reports and other essential info helping you understand which market places offer the best chances of appreciation. He will always be an idol to me. Join his buying tour if you have the money. This is where Mr. Garrison takes you into the actual "market places" with the best chances of growth and goes over the evaluation and buying process "hands-on". The reviews are always fantastic and I'm confident that it will be a priceless experience for you!

***

http://www.realestatetiming.com

Robert Campbell falls into the same category as Marc Stephen Garrison. He specializes in researching market places to determine the best chances for appreciation and cash flow. His book, "**Timing the Real Estate Market**", is a must read. It's actually perfect to read right after my book because he goes into much more depth on the importance of locations and various economic indicators that help determine housing prices. Go to his site, read his literature and find out what other authors are saying about him. Get his "**Market Momentum Charting Software**" for free as a special bonus and stay ahead of the competition from that point on!

***

FORECLOSURE SEARCHES & CONTINUED EDUCATION

http://www.realtytrac.com

This site offers a great tool for accessing information on foreclosures and REO's (bank-owned) properties. The monthly fee is only $19.95 and they really keep their listings up to date which is a "big plus" for any companies offering foreclosure search engines. Join for a free 7 day trial, read their testimonials and then search away!

***

Before doing this I suggest you let the 2 extremely intelligent ladies below educate you on the topics of:

- **pre-foreclosures**
- **Foreclosures**
- **short sales**

http://www.texasrealestateclub.com

Dwan Bent-Twyford and Sharon Restrepo are both rather amazing individuals. They both got started in real estate investing because of tragic circumstances they couldn't control or predict. They have gone on to be some of most successful investors out there using the seminar circuit to "spread the word" about the real estate investing techniques that have made them fortunes! I suggest you purchase their kits on the topics above if you want a step-by-step guide to these advanced real estate investing techniques.

The site above also has numerous free resources you can benefit and learn from. Check the other areas of the site for topics that may be of interest to you.

***

LEASE TO OWN RESOURCES

http://www.l2p.com

Jeff Beaubien has created an excellent site giving you everything you need to understand the profitable "lease to purchase" investment technique. Start with the basics by clicking on **How to Lease Purchase**. Then review **FREE Report Winning in the Lease Purchase Business**. From there you can get inspired by his Success Stories and take advantage of his **Tips, Strategies & Secrets**. After that you can visit his **Chat Board** and finish off with **Frequently Asked Questions**.

You have to get the following because they're extremely beneficial:

- Free monthly newsletter
- Free downloads (real estate calculators, and all kinds of other interesting stuff)

- Lease Purchase handbook (it's $147 but well worth it*)

His handbook is very easy to understand and I feel like he's taking me "step-by-step" through every part of the lease to own process. This is the main reason I feel that it's a "must have" for any beginning-intermediate investor.

***

http://www.hotpropertysolutions.co.nz

Brian Gibbons really knows his stuff when it comes to lease to own investing. His site offers various ways for sellers and buyers to take advantage of this real estate ownership option. This is his marketing strategy live and in the flesh. He mentors students on occasion and offers resources you must take advantage of. I would suggest visiting the site and looking at the following:

- **INVESTOR INFO**—he offers a great way to make a solid 15-33% return on investment by being a silent partner in the deals he coordinates (this is perfect for beginning investors that still believe in diversifying their investment strategies and letting experts manage their capital)
- **FREE REPORTS**—lease to own basics and more!
- **FREE DOWNLOADS**—agreements, applications, etc.

Brian is really a good guy who offers a lot of his time for free and truly believes that you have to "give in order to receive!" Go to his site and see what I'm talking about.

***

LEGAL AND TAX ADVISOR RESOURCES

LEGAL

http://www.sutlaw.com

Garrett Sutton has been a tremendous asset for me. He's helped me set up entities, consulted with me on specific strategies within my game plan, and gave me priceless advice on various real estate and business related topics. He's an idol for me being part of the "RICH DAD CIRCLE OF ADVISORS". He defines integrity, success and the willingness to help other investors out in their quest for success! He's personally a main advisor for developing my intellectual property. Check out the following on his site:

- **Subscribe to the SuccessDNA newsletter**
- **Learn about Products we offer**

These 2 links will give you everything you need to know about how you can take advantage of his knowledge and expertise as a consultant to some of the most successful people out there. I recommend that you read his books and take advantage of his other product offerings!

***

http://www.prepaidlegal.com

The folks at Pre-Paid Legal Services®, Inc. have created a unique opportunity where you can utilize their network of attorney's across the nation or become an affiliate and start a part-time business! In fact, you can be both a client and a partner. Click on the following links to learn more:

- **Legal Service Plans**
- **Free Legal Information**

They're listed on the NYSE exchange (PPD) and they've grown tremendously since they first started back in 1972. Their monthly free is very reasonable and they offer fantastic customer support. Check them out and let me know what you think!

***

TAX

http://www.taxloopholes.com

Diane Kennedy is another member of the RICH DAD CIRCLE OF ADVISORS. She offers tons of advice on tax preparation and strategies. Check out her site and make sure to click on the following:

- **TAX LOOPHOLE EDUCATIONAL PRODUCTS**
- **DKA ACCOUNTING**

The first link will lead you to her product offerings. You can't go wrong with her classic book titled: LOOPHOLES OF THE RICH. I can't even tell you how much I've learned from this one book. It's literally saved me thousands of dollars. Her company, DKA ACCOUNTING, offers consultation and educational resources helping you achieve your goals and objectives with the assistance of a true "professional". Join her free newsletter and take advantage of her free tips as well. You can never have enough education on the topic of: SAVING MONEY ON TAXES. Visit her site and you'll see what I'm talking about!

www.savinggreen.com

In today's world we know the average American works the first 4 to 6 months of each year just to pay their taxes. Paying one's fair share of taxes is our responsibility, overpaying is not! Saving Green, Inc. offers a **free** second opinion. They take your tax returns from the past 3 years and review them with

updated tax laws from the IRS. Most people don't know that brand new tax laws can be applied back up to 3 years. Further, they look for omissions or errors and determine whether or not you are entitled to a refund. NO REFUND! NO CHARGE!

The service depends on finding you money and receiving referrals. On average they find 70% of their customers between $6,000—$10,000...enough for a down payment on another piece of real estate!

***

INVESTOR ASSOCIATIONS

www.realestateinvesting.com

Go to this site and click on **Investor Associations** located on the left hand column. From this list you can pick your individual state and find various investor groups available for your support. Again, these are great places to meet potential mentors, advisors, and valuable team members. Here are other sites you can visit to find even more investor associations:

www.creonline.com

Go to *resources* and click on **real estate clubs**. From here you can locate clubs within your own state and call, email or fax over an application to become a member. You have to go to a few different clubs and start constructing your team. This is another great place to get started. Here are a few more resources for locating investor associations:

www.reitoolbelt.com
⇓

Click on *community* then go to **REI Clubs***

www.resultsnow.com
⇓

Click on **Real Estate Investor Associations** on the left hand side of the page

Well, I think this should give you plenty of resources to start with! I actually have others but I will leave this for a very specialized "follow up book" in the near future. Thanks again for all of your attention and continued support. Don't hesitate to email me with any questions or concerns at: **sales@reismart.com**. I will be happy to help my readers out in any way possible!

ACKNOWLEDGEMENTS

So many people have been influential in the creation of this book. I want to thank my wife and best friend, Robbin Petreeko, for all of the love, support, and patience provided since the start of this project. This book is dedicated to you.

I thank my **Mom & Dad** for instilling the principles necessary for me to become successful, hard working, and appreciative. They would do anything to help me out and believed I could achieve anything if I put my mind to it.

I wouldn't be where I am today without the mentoring from **Terrence Gray**, my friend and business partner. We now continue to learn from each other but I still remember the day when he first introduced "Rich Dad, Poor Dad" to me. It changed my life from that point on. Terrence believed in me from day 1 and I have the utmost respect for him as a friend and a business professional.

Paul Dell'Aquila is a true friend, as well as a business partner for all of our corporations' real estate holdings. We are a perfect team. I wish we met about 2 years ago. Here's to acquiring the next 100 properties! Thanks again for all of your help in stressful, unpredictable times.

Gabi Golan gets an enormous thank you for having to hear all of my stories for the past 3+ years...good and bad! Gabi is an amazing friend that would do anything for me. He is an extremely successful, dedicated individual that could achieve whatever he desires. I still promise to "recruit him" one day when the time is right. He will make a great leader for his own company!

Candy & Herb—you both have showed me tremendous support and would do anything for Robbin and myself. I idolize your lifestyle but I respect your accomplishments, hard work and modesty even more!

Robbie—you took us in before we made the transition to our new home and made our lives easier during times of uncertainty. I still can't thank you enough for the hospitality you displayed to me. Thank you for always being there for us.

Bub & Pop—You would support me no matter what destination I chose. You have given me an endless supply of positive energy and enthusiasm throughout my life. I cherish your dedication, faith, and zest for life.

Rami—this whole company would still be in its infancy without your help and guidance...you're a very talented individual and I can't wait to work on our next "project" together!

SPECIAL THANKS

Mike Schwartz...you've been a leader, mentor and a friend since we first met. You've taught me everything I know about sales and I owe you tremendously for this. You are a genuine, hard working person dedicated to your family, friends & career.

Bill Genard & Rob Hammer...We've known each other since our days of cleaning floors at PowerHouse Gym in Bridgewater. I wouldn't take back those days for the world. We've had many great experiences together through our times of growing and developing. We've done plenty of stupid stuff along the way but recognized our mistakes and made them into victories. You guys believed in me when nobody else did. You told me I would be going places when I was filled with self-doubt and negativity. You let me be myself and respected my decisions. You guys will always be true friends. I can't wait to get you guys involved in some future joint ventures!

ABOUT THE AUTHOR

Jon Petreeko's ultimate goal is to sell over 1 million copies of his book, **Real Estate Investing Smart from the Start**© within 2 years. His primary focus is providing clients the level of excellence they demand. He's experienced first hand that real estate investing is an extremely broad and confusing topic. Many beginners suffer from "information overload".

Too many investors will give up because they don't really know when to take their first step. They need someone to give them the "play-by-play" without any details left out. They want someone they can relate to. They want someone to teach them through true stories of "failure and success" on various real estate investing topics. They want to know how this technique can assist them in achieving their real estate investing goals.

Real Estate Investing Smart from the Start© is an ideal place to start your education on this broad topic. It also serves as an invaluable resource and learning guide for the intermediate investor. Many experienced investor's want to brush-up on various techniques and procedures essential in acquiring profitable investment properties with the greatest chances of appreciation possible.

Many investors will benefit tremendously from this book. It's the main reason why Jon Petreeko chooses to share his experiences and successes with as many people as possible. His goal is to make you successful in achieving your goals!

He states: "you should never write about something you're not absolutely passionate about!" Real estate investing is his passion. His dream is to help educate as many people as possible on this topic and really make a difference in their overall "success-building" plans.

Help him achieve this by emailing him specific topics that you would like to see covered on his website and product offerings in the future. He can be reached at: **sales@reismart.com**.

ACCOMPLISHMENTS:

Jon Petreeko is an investor that uses businesses and real estate to achieve his primary investing objectives and goals.

He's a principal and part of the board of directors for **CPN** (http://www.cpndr.com/); a company offering administration and consultation services for physicians interested in converting to a concierge-based practice.

- He's also on the board of directors for **Time+ NY**; a payroll administration and human resources solution provider for companies of all sizes nationwide.

- In addition to his book, **Real Estate Investing Smart from the Start©**, Jon Petreeko owns **REIsmart, LLC**. This company is dedicated to increasing an investor's education step-by-step on various real estate related topics. These topics are required in order to increase the potential of achieving wealth and success.

- He has equity ownership in numerous corporations that maintain and profit from real estate holdings throughout the nation.

- Jon Petreeko also works as a sales consultant for **New Horizons Worldwide**, the # 1 provider of computer training solutions for businesses and consumers across the globe. He maintains loyalty to this company for the sales and marketing education it has provided and helped him develop throughout the years. He continues to earn "vital business experience" from key mentors within the company.

Jon Petreeko resides in Northern New Jersey with his wife Robbin, who has been an integral part of his game plan since day 1. He cannot stress the importance of having someone in your life that will follow your dreams and support your goals. His success is directly related to the positive influence that Robbin has had on his life.